EVANS 78

EVANS 78

SWANSEA
THOSE WERE THE DAYS!

South Wales **Evening Post**

SWANSEA
THOSE WERE THE DAYS!

by David Roberts

breedon **books**
PUBLISHING

First published in Great Britain in 2002 by
The Breedon Books Publishing Company Limited
Breedon House, 3 The Parker Centre,
Derby, DE21 4SZ

ISBN 1 85983 334 9

Printed and bound by Butler & Tanner, Frome, Somerset,
England.

Cover printing by Lawrence-Allen Colour Printers,
Weston-super-Mare, Somerset.

CONTENTS

An Appreciation

This book would not have been possible without the valued assistance of readers of the *South Wales Evening Post* and the many residents of Swansea who submitted their own personal images of days gone by. Particular thanks are due to:

John, Alfred and the late S. N. Peake,
David and Eiluned Govier,
Ken and Mollie Reeves,
Harold and Evelyn Phillipart,
Julie Jones,
Tom Coleman,
Dan Morgan,
Paul Murray,
William Pressdee,
Tony Cottle,
Ken and Marie John,
Barrie Griffiths,
John Feldman,
Peter Ridgewell,
Des Roberts,
Michael Jones,
Bob Rees,
Peter Fenwick,
Sid Kidwell,
David Beynon and Cheryl Roberts.

FOREWORD

THE publication of *Swansea – Those Were The Days* is a remarkable achievement. Not only is it the fifth such book to appear in consecutive years, but it also brings the number of pictures from the past now drawn together to more than 2,000.

Continuing to depict much of Swansea's social history it follows the successful pattern of previous books in a series that has earned a proud place on bookshelves far and wide.

Swansea – Those Were The Days has resulted in a further, fascinating crop of illustrations of faces, places and events from days past. Like its predecessors the book owes much to the willingness and enthusiasm of people to participate in a significant record that can be shared by all.

It contains a memory-jerking miscellany that will undoubtedly provide much pleasure. The *South Wales Evening Post* is delighted to be associated with David Roberts in this latest evocative trip down memory lane.

George Edwards,
Editor,
South Wales Evening Post.

FROM EARLIEST BEGINNINGS TO MODERN TIMES

AS WALES' first and finest seaside city, Swansea is no stranger to the attentions of visitors. It has entertained an endless procession of them from its earliest beginnings right up to modern times. Apart from pre-historic arrivals, the Romans, the Vikings and then the Normans all came calling at some point in much the same way as today's tourists, except that in earlier times many stayed and influenced the city's evolution.

Much of Swansea's boundary is shared with the sea, so it is not surprising that was the preferred approach for those early callers – and one of the attractions for today's.

It is also the prime reason for the development of Swansea as a port – in the early 19th century the principal one in Wales, the third largest in Britain – and though this superiority has waned, its links with the sea have not. Much of the old dockland area has given birth to an award-winning maritime quarter complete with marina.

On land, the arrival of the Normans in the 11th century and the early settlement around Swansea's 12th-century castle represent the start of its growth. As a small market town and port, its fortunes ebbed and flowed as regularly as the tide that lapped its shores until the 18th century and the mining of the huge coal reserves beneath the surrounding countryside.

Such ready supplies of the mineral soon turned Swansea into a world leader for metal smelting and other industrial processes. Even faster was the growth of its population and urban spread – the first answering the call of employment and the second the need to house those who came for that work.

The legacy of this prosperity and rapid growth was the industrial wasteland of the Lower Swansea Valley – polluted by heavy metals and despoiled by waste tips. But this was just a fresh challenge for the proud community, and the area was transformed into a successful arena for 21st century business – and a recreational asset – Swansea Enterprise Park.

Urban development between two World Wars pushed out from the centre and since 1945 suburban sprawl has both swallowed up open countryside and overtaken existing communities.

Wartime bombing saw the heart of the old town of Swansea with its cosy, narrow streets wiped out and the eventual birth of much that can be seen today.

The modern city has nearly 250,000 inhabitants, and, through their labours, continues to prosper.

David Roberts
2002

STREET SCENES

Life was slower in Oxford Street when this picture was taken in 1900 – unlike the frantic pace of later years.

Looking up Constitution Hill, with its short-lived 3ft 6in gauge funicular tramway. The trams were powered by an engine house at the top and passed in a short loop. It ran from 1898 until 1901.

Motor vehicles had yet to make their mark in the Wind Street of 1904, but it was still a busy thoroughfare with horse-drawn vehicles carrying all kinds of goods up and down.

King Edward Road, looking eastwards towards Brynymor Road, 1905. The approaching tram, tramway and overhead cables were all new to the district.

The tramway terminus at High Street, looking up towards the railway station, with the Hotel Cameron on the right, 1905.

The view up a bunting-filled Wind Street, 1904.

Tramcar No. 4 leaves the terminus in High Street for Cwmbwrla on a wet day, 1905.

The imposing Swansea Post Office building, Wind Street, 1905.

Looking up St Helen's Road, near its junction with Brynymor Road, 1906. Swansea General Hospital can be seen in the background.

Tram No.66 at Alexandra Road terminus was on loan to Swansea Tramways when this picture was being taken in High Street, 1906. The workman up the ladder working on the street light had already attracted attention from onlookers.

The Salisbury Club and Hotel Metropole with its curved portico overhanging Wind Street, 1906.

St Helen's Road, looking eastwards, 1906.

Swansea Library, Alexandra Road, 1907.

King Edward Road, winter, 1907.

A double deck tram, car No.32 heads into town along Oxford Street, 1908. The market with its imposing domed entrance can be seen on the right.

The Glynn Vivian art gallery, Alexandra Road, 1909.

Looking eastwards along Oxford Street and into Temple Street, 1910.

Looking down High Street into Castle Street, 1909.

Wind Street, 1914. On the right, Swansea's main Post Office building.

The bridge linking Victoria Park with Swansea sands. It was opened in 1914 and this summertime picture was taken in 1916.

Oxford Street showing Swansea's famous Empire Theatre, early 1920s. The Carlton Cinema is just beyond it.

A 1920 Wind Street looking up towards Castle Bailey. Dominating the scene in the centre is the Ben Evans department store.

Wind Street, looking into Castle Bailey and up to Castle Street with the familiar outline of Castle Buildings, 1922.

Temple Street, which ran between Oxford Street and Castle Street, 1925, showing the post office which later became the offices of the *South Wales Evening Post*. Of course, they later moved to Adelaide Street.

Wind Street, 1928.

The premises of Webster's complete funeral furnishers, Calvert Street, early 1930s.

Swansea Liberal Club, Wind Street, early 1930s.

An early 1930s view of St Mary's Parish Church.

St Mary Street, early 1930s.

The London & North Western Hotel, Rutland Street, 1937. Damaged in the Three Nights, Blitz of February, 1941 it was later renamed the Clyne Valley Hotel.

The Grand Theatre,
Singleton Street,
1935.

The view from the roof of Swansea Guildhall, looking towards Mumbles, 1937. Swansea Bay station can be seen on the left along with the Patti Pavilion, Victoria Park and St Helen's sports ground.

Calvert Street, looking eastwards towards the back of Ben Evans store, 1937.

Firemen's hoses lay in Calvert Street alongside St Mary's Church and smoke still rises from the ruins of Ben Evans department store after the Three Nights' Blitz. The bomb-damaged properties on the left are now the site of Littlewoods store.

This post-war panorama of central Swansea, 1947, shows just how much wartime damage had been done to the town's heart.

A view of The Kingsway, 1951. The No Waiting sign on the roadway in front perhaps offered a hint of restrictions to come. The Plaza cinema is on the left. The façade next to the Plaza disguises three Nissen huts used as premises for war-damaged shops.

Swansea Guildhall, May 30, 1951.

Looking down The Kingsway towards St Helen's Road, 1951. Bomb-damaged Dynevor School is visible on the right. Much commercial redevelopment had yet to come.

Roofless, but still standing proud, Dynevor School, a victim of the wartime blitz, pictured in 1951. It was the only city centre school to survive until July 2002.

Construction work under way on The Kingsway near its junction with Upper Union Street. The popular Burlington restaurant and café is clearly visible, 1951. Spot the name painted on its roof.

Wind Street, early 1950s, showing C.A. Sanders' tobacconist store at No.1 Wind Street and next door, the Duke Hotel.

A pattern of new roadways begins to emerge from the rubble of the war-blitzed town centre, 1951.

The station in Rutland Street opposite the departure point for the Mumbles Train, 1951.

St Mary's Parish Church in 1951 – nearly 10 years after German bombs had reduced it to a shell.

As Swansea began to rebuild after the war this was the 1951 view from Orchard Street, across College Street towards Woolworth's High Street store and on the right Castle Buildings, Castle Street.

A lone workman sweeps the cobbled forecourt of Victoria Station, shortly before its closure in June 1964.

The view eastwards along The Kingsway, 1957.

Salubrious Passage, linking Wind Street and York Street, 1959.

Looking westwards along The Kingsway, 1956. The new C&A store was for many a fashion mecca.

A 1954 aerial view of the new Swansea that rose from the wartime ashes.

A springtime view across Castle Gardens neatly frames this view of St Mary's Parish Church, 1969.

The Post Office tower rises up from The Strand to dominate the ruins of Swansea Castle, 1974. In the foreground is the fountain, which graced Castle Gardens until it was moved to the Botanical Gardens at Singleton after repeated attacks by vandals.

Oystermouth Road at its junction with St Helen's Road, 1974. Once, on the right where a bus and car are parked ran the Mumbles Railway, while the raised embankment carried the Swansea-Shrewsbury railway line.

All that remains of the site of Victoria Station, June 1974. Swansea Leisure Centre and its car park occupy the site now. On the right can be seen some of the arches that carried railway lines across the city.

Construction work under way on Swansea Leisure Centre, 1975.

A late-1970s aerial view of Swansea, showing Vetch Field, home of Swansea City AFC, above it the Quadrant bus station and above that the Quadrant shopping centre.

Work under way to clear the material that had been used to fill in the South Dock in preparation for its rebirth as part of Swansea Marina, 1980. The building on the right became Swansea's Maritime and Industrial Museum.

Work continues excavating material from the South Dock basin, March 6, 1981, in preparation for its development as a marina.

A 1980s aerial view of the construction of the St David's Centre and the nearby multi-storey car park.

A night-time view looking up Portland Street, 1981.

Mount Pleasant hospital, 1983. The building was formerly Tawe Lodge and the Union Workhouse.

Fabian Way and the Cape Horner public house, early 1980s. The bridge in the centre of the picture carried a rail link into the docks from the Neath and Swansea valleys.

Traffic was diverted on Sunday, October 27, 1985, while workmen removed the railway bridge that crossed Fabian Way near the entrance to Swansea Docks.

A mid-1980s panorama of the mouth of the River Tawe, showing the site later occupied by Sainsbury's supermarket.

Meet the People

Members of Tabernacle Bible Class, 1914.

Residents and friends of Heol Tirdu, Cwmrhydyceirw, Morriston who rallied round to raise the sum of £10 19s 1d in aid of Swansea's wartime Spitfire aircraft fund, 1940.

Members of Sketty Baptist Church
Sunday School, late 1940s.

A real get-together. The Martin family of Port Tennant gather at the end of David Williams Terrace, 1945.

Members of Manselton Ladies Guild, early 1950s.

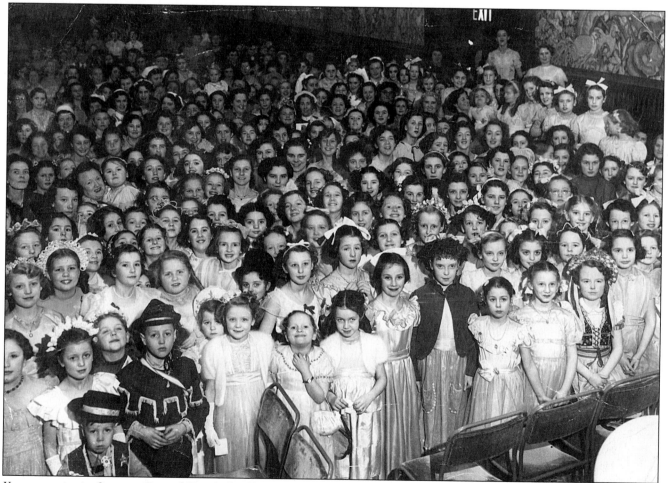

Young guests at a Swansea General Hospital Ball at the Brangwyn Hall, 1951. The hospital, in St Helen's Road, closed its wards around 1962-3.

Colleagues of the Windsmoor clothing factory at Fforestfach at their annual dance, 1952.

Proprietors and staff of Waynes Stores, Uplands at their annual dinner and dance at the Mackworth Hotel, 1952. The store was run by brothers Fred, Will, Sid and Bert Wayne. Sid's son Robin still runs florists in Uplands.

The Pier Hotel, Mumbles was the venue for the annual Christmas dinner dance of the South Wales Builders Supply Company, 1953. The main builders' merchants in Swansea, the company had two large showrooms in Wind Street and an extensive yard at Fforestfach.

Young friends from Llwyncethin Road, Gendros rest their weary legs, 1953.

Members of Swansea Youth Council at Kilvrough Manor, Parkmill, Gower, 1955.

Friends enjoy a night out at the Pier Hotel, Mumbles, 1956.

Four young residents of Gendros pose for the cameraman in their Sunday best, 1956.

Members of Townhill Community Centre, enjoy a get-together, late 1950s.

The Brunswick Street section of the South Wales Transport Company's Christmas party at the Mackworth Hotel, 1959.

Members of St Michael's Church, Manselton at a Cymryr Groes – welcome event – June 1959.

A group of children at Bonymaen Community Centre, 1960.

Staff of office equipment distributors Robert Kerr, Imperial typewriter agents at Alexandra Road, Swansea during their annual dinner, 1960.

Railway workers and their partners enjoy a night out, early 1960s.

Time to relax for these employees of the Mettoy toy factory at Fforestfach, 1961.

Regulars at The Tredegar Arms, Sandfields, enjoy a pint, May 1962.

A group of Swansea railway workers were joined by their Margam, Port Talbot counterparts for this special dinner, 1963.

Waitresses from the Dragon Hotel, Belle Vue Way, headed off to the Caswell Bay Hotel for their annual dinner, February 1964.

Staff of Swansea Teleservices Ltd., at a celebration function, 1964.

Members of the congregation of St Michael's Church, Manselton, at a special party held to celebrate its 60th anniversary on January 27, 1966.

GPO telephonists in the mood for a great night out, Christmas, 1968.

A night out for White Watch at Swansea Fire Station, Grove Place, 1972.

The Caswell Bay hotel, Gower was the venue for this gathering of committee members of the Glanmor club and their wives, 1972.

Sixth floor colleagues of the DVLC at Clase at their annual Christmas lunch at The Pines Club, Treboeth, 1976.

Singleton hospital staff raise funds with a charity pram push, mid-1980s.

AROUND AND ABOUT

A stopping point on the Mumbles Railway at Blackpill, early 1890s. The sign to the right is an invitation to call at a flower, fruit and tea gardens.

The Mill at Blackpill, early 1900s.

Sketty Road, Sketty, looking towards the Cross, 1904.

Brynmill Park on a summer Sunday afternoon, 1904.

A view over Morriston from Bryn Rock about 1905. The spire of Tabernacle Church points skyward, copied by countless industrial chimneys that fill the area now occupied by Swansea Enterprise Park.

Landore, like much of the rest of the lower Swansea Valley was a cauldron of industrial activity when this picture was taken in 1907. The railway viaduct can be seen in the centre and Hafod tip on the right.

Heavy flooding near Norton Road, West Cross, following a thunderstorm on July 22, 1907.

Tranquil times at Cwmdonkin Park, Uplands, 1907.

Blackpill, 1908. The first property on the right is the post office and next to it the village police station.

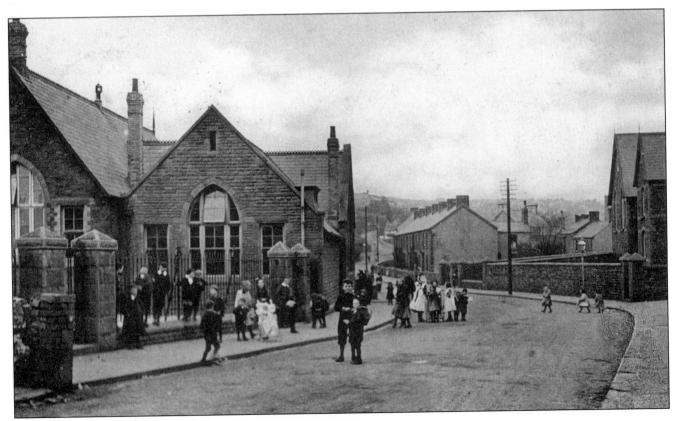

School's out at Brynhyfryd, 1908.

A 1908 view over part of Treboeth. Gwyrosydd School, Penlan now stands on the open space towards the bottom right of the picture.

A group gathers in front of Siloam chapel, Killay, 1908.

Tramway repair work under way near St John's Church, Woodfield Street, Morriston, in 1910 amuses a group of onlookers.

Mason's Road, Kingsbridge, Gorseinon, 1910. It later became West Street.

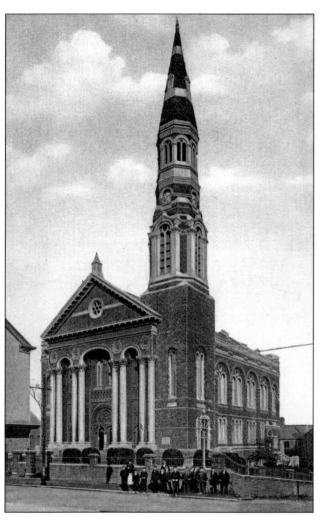

Tabernacle Congregational
Chapel, Woodfield Street,
Morriston, 1910.

Looking down Pentrepoeth Road, Morriston, 1914.

Two young girls quench their thirst from the ornate, metal-cupped fountain alongside the lake at Brynmill Park, 1915.

A view across Morriston Park, 1916.

Windmill Terace, St Thomas, 1916.

Burlais Brook, Cwmbwrla, Hafod. Later culverted, houses now stand here. The brook marked the old boundary of Swansea town and figured in the 'beating the bounds' ceremony.

Brynmill Park in the late 1920s.

St James's Gardens, Uplands, 1929.

The Mexico Fountain Inn at the junction of Tip Row with Neath Road, Hafod, November 1931.

Neath Road, Hafod on a murky winter's day, 1932. The tram lines have just left Prince of Wales Road.

The Smith's Crisps factory seemingly in the middle of nowhere at Cadle, 1949. Now the Portmead housing development fills the open fields to its right, Tesco Extra the fields across the road and Cadle primary school in the centre foreground has been demolished.

They built the houses first and the roadway and pavement followed later. These houses at Llwyncethin Road, Gendros had just received their first occupants when this picture was taken in 1951.

Looking along Dillwyn Road, towards the Cross, Sketty, 1952.

Port Tennant Road, Port Tennant, mid-1950s.

The start of construction of the new depot yard at the South Wales Transport Company's sprawling depot at Ravenhill, 1957.

An aerial view of the Bible College of Wales, Derwen Fawr, late 1950s.

A close up the Bible College, 1960.

A fascinating frosty, winter-morning view down Margaret Street, Port Tennant, taking in the cranes and warehouses of Swansea Docks behind, late 1950s.

Dillwyn Road, Sketty, looking towards the Cross, 1968. On-street parking was by now becoming more difficult.

May 19, 1976 saw the demolition by explosives of this bridge, which carried the A48 between Llangyfelach and Penllergaer, to make way for the construction of the M4 motorway

The Driver and Vehicle Licensing Centre towers over the rest of Clase, Friday, May 1, 1981. Beacons View Road curves down through the centre of the picture.

Nothing moved when snow choked Brynhyfryd Square, Brynhyfryd – along with the remainder of Swansea – in the winter of 1982.

Neath Road, Hafod, looking towards Dyfatty with road widening work under way to the left, 1982.

Pleasant Row, Brynhyfryd, 1983. It has since been demolished to make way for redevelopment.

Beaufort Industrial estate has developed extensively since this aerial snapshot was taken in 1983. The garages that line Neath Road can be seen along with the Swansea Valley by-pass. In the middle distance open land can be seen where Morfa Athletics Stadium stands today.

SPECIAL DAYS

A send off for the bride and groom after a 1908 Gower wedding.

Kathleen Morgan, daughter of the Morgan family who ran a successful butchery business in Swansea market on the day she became Mrs Pepper, 1920s.

A typical mid-1920s Swansea wedding.

Wedding cars wait outside All Saints Church, Oystermouth, in 1926 ready to whisk a bride and groom away to their reception. The vehicles are Humbers and a Dodge, owned by W. Presdee, of Stanley Street, Mumbles.

The official opening of Gowerton church hall, January 3, 1929.

It really was a special day for the 1930s bride who was carried to the church in this spectacularly decorated limousine.

A funeral cortège arrives at Mynyddbach cemetery, mid-1930s. Its size may indicate the funeral of someone of prominence.

One of a number of GI brides married in wartime Swansea pictured with her groom, believed to be from Chicago, late 1942.

Residents of Watkin Street, Mount Pleasant, celebrate VE Day with a street party, 1945.

VE Day celebrations – fancy dress style – for youngsters who attended Tabernacle branch Sunday school, Ynysforgan, 1945.

Residents of Penygraig Road, Townhill gather for their VE Day party, 1945.

Peter Fenwick and his bride Pru Thomas after their wedding at St Catherine's Church, Gorseinon, 1946.

GI bride Megan Thomas and her American serviceman groom Frank Walters after their wedding at St Catherine's Church, Gorseinon, 1946.

Members of Swansea British Legion branch take part in an Armistice Day parade, November 9, 1947. They are seen marching along Northampton Place which later became The Kingsway.

Sea Rangers and Girl Guides of St Jude's Church, on parade at Terrace Road, 1948.

Youngsters of David Street, Cwmbwrla, received a visit from the mayor and mayoress, on this early-1950s day.

Swansea Town soccer stars Ivor Allchurch and Trevor Ford congratulate colleague Ray Daniels after his wedding to Joyce Richards at Tabernacle Chapel, Waun Wen, 1950.

Mr Howell, chairman of the South Wales Electricity Board turns the key to officially open the board's welfare club at Heathfield, 1952.

Some of the congregation of St Paul's Church, St Helen's Road gather after a service to commemorate the Coronation of Queen Elizabeth II, 1953.

Blackpill residents gather for a party to mark the Coronation of Queen Elizabeth II, 1953.

Bride and groom Alf and Brenda Whitby leave Swansea railway station to start their honeymoon on August 14, 1954.

Officers of the Royal Ancient Order of Buffaloes at their Wind Street club, mid-1950s.

Stan McLaughlan and Joy Thomas with guests at their St Peter's Church, Cockett, wedding, 1955.

Members of the congregation at the re-consecration service at St Mary's Church, Swansea, May 31, 1958.

This was the day the circus came to town and paraded its elephants along Oystermouth Road, opposite St Helen's Sports Ground, despite the rain, late 1950s.

Guests at a Guildhall luncheon to mark the end of the Mumbles Railway, January 5, 1960.

A moment of fun for these choirboys at St Peter's Church, Cockett, in 1967 when they were joined by the late Sir Harry Secombe. Harry's brother Fred is the clergyman in the pulpit.

Student nurses at Park Beck nurses home on the first day of their course, 1967.

There was no shortage of tasty fare when residents of Wern Fawr Road, Port Tennant, sat down to the street party they held to celebrate the Silver Jubilee of Queen Elizabeth II, 1977.

Party fun to celebrate the wedding of the Prince of Wales to Lady Diana, 1981.

Carnival capers for staff of Singleton Hospital as their float waits in Cambrian Place to join the parade, early 1980s.

SHOPPING SPOTLIGHT

The Co-operative store at Treboeth with some of its staff outside, early 1900s.

John Williams cycle store, Alexandra Road, 1907.

F.J. Jenkins, hosiery specialists, 33 Oxford Street, 1912.

If you wanted your picture taken in 1905 you may well have headed for this photographer's studio in narrow Castle Street.

Parsons seed merchant's premises and Myrddin Davies, cash chemist were just two of the many stores that helped Oxford Street thrive in the early 1920s.

High Street was a busy shopping thoroughfare in the 1920s. The famous Lewis Lewis Store is on the left.

The ironmongers store in Loughor Road, Gorseinon, 1920.

F.W. Woolworth's store, High Street, 1925.

John Mitchell outside his electrical store, Woodfield Street, Morriston, 1935.

Woolworth's High Street store with its cafeteria suffered badly in the Three Nights Blitz in February 1941. Here scaffolding supports some of what remained.

Penclawdd cocklewomen sell their wares outside war-damaged Swansea market, 1947.

In 1947, a decent fish and chip lunch at the cafe here at Swansea market cost 2s 11d (less than 15p).

Shoppers in College Street, 1947.

Swansea's post-war temporary market, 1951. Stalls were made from packing cases used to ship wartime aircraft through the docks.

Staff of Oliver's shoe shop ready and waiting for customers, Oxford Street, 1953.

Post-war reconstruction brought plenty of new shops, like these, with offices above circling The Kingsway roundabout, 1957.

Two stallholders in Swansea's newly-opened modern market take time out for a cuppa, 1960.

Part of upper High Street, mid-1970s.

A wet 1981 night-time view of Oxford Street showing John Menzies stationery store, Top Shop, and to the far left, the Cooperative store, both now gone.

Queuing for bargains the day Woolworth's closed their High Street store, July 1986.

PUPIL POWER

A group of Gorseinon Infants School children, 1927.

Standard 2B Gorseinon Girls School, 1929.

Girls of St Thomas Junior School, 1932.

Waun Wen Boys, Junior School, 1937.

Terrace Road School celebrates the Coronation of King George V, 1937.

Pupils of Waunarlwydd School, 1937.

Cwm School, Winch Wen, June 1940.

Waunarlwydd School, 1940.

Pupils Brian Evans and Keith Davies painting a mural on the wall of Hafod Boys' School, 1947.

Children from Parkmill School, Gower pictured on a visit to King Arthur's Stone, Cefn Bryn, summer 1948.

Girls at Christchurch School all dressed up in traditional Welsh costume for St David's Day, 1950.

St Helen's School, Vincent Street, early 1950s.

An outdoor PE lesson for girls at St Helen's Junior mixed school, 1951.

Staff and pupils at Llwyn Y Bryn School watching a netball match from the school verandah, March 30, 1951.

Form 5A, Llwyn Y Bryn School, on the school terrace, 1951.

Cwmbwrla Infants School, 1952.

Cwmbwrla Junior School, 1952.

A class at Oxford Street Boys School, with teachers and headmaster, 1954.

Terrace Road Primary School was one of the first to have new-style PE apparatus in its hall, 1954.

Peniel Green School, Llansamlet, 1955.

Pupils of St Helen's Secondary Modern School at the Brangwyn Hall, October 24, 1958.

Birchgrove Nursery School, 1958.

A first year form at Dynevor School, 1959.

Pupils of Dillwyn House, Terrace Road School, 1959.

Powys School, 1959.

Brynmill Junior School pupils at the botanical gardens, Singleton Park, 1959.

Form 5 Gregg High School, 1962.

Blaenymaes Primary School, 1963.

Manselton Infants School pupils hold their Harvest Festival service, October, 1964.

Brynmill School, 1964.

Parklands Primary School, Sketty, 1966.

Brynhyfryd Junior School, 1966.

Manselton Infants School, 1966.

Brynhyfryd Junior School pupils on a visit to Swansea Airport, July 7, 1967.

Sketty School, July 1967.

Cwmbwrla Junior School, 1969.

Morriston Boys Junior School, 1969.

Morriston Boys Junior School, 1971.

Manselton Comprehensive School, February 1971.

Manselton Junior Comprehensive School, 1972.

Dynevor School prefects, 1972.

Penlan Comprehensive School, 1973.

Manselton Infants School, October 1975.

Pupils of Gors Primary School celebrate the Silver Jubilee of Queen Elizabeth II, 1977.

Mumbles and Gower

Looking down on the junction of Mumbles Road and Newton Road, mid-1800s.

Oyster boats lay within the pool at Mumbles, waiting for the tide, 1886.

A view across Mumbles looking towards Swansea, around 1895.

A view across Mumbles towards the recently completed pier about 1900.

The Quarry, Mumbles, early 1900s.

Newton village 1905.

The Gower Inn, Parkmill, 1907.

The mill at Parkmill, 1910.

The parade and gardens, Mumbles, 1910.

A fascinating view of Newton, 1910.

Camping fields at Limeslade, 1920.

Langland Bay with its rows of beach tents and huts and behind them, the convalescent home, 1930s.

Bungalows at Limeslade, 1939.

Murton Church and Post Office, 1941.

Limeslade Bay, late 1940s.

The Osborne Hotel, Langland, late 1940s.

Caswell Bay, late 1940s.

Parkmill from the air, showing Shepherd's Stores on the right, 1947.

The railed steps between Langland and Groves Avenue, 1948.

Underhill Park, Mumbles, viewed from Newton Villas late 1940s.

The Mermaid Hotel,
Southend, Mumbles,
early 1950s.

The Gladstone restaurant, Southend, Mumbles,
early 1950s.

Three Cliffs Bay, Gower, early 1950s.

Post Office Corner, Newton, early 1950s.

Oxwich Bay, early 1950s.

Mumbles
Conservative Club,
1952.

Caswell Bay, mid-1950s.

Caswell Hill, mid-1950s. The field edged by caravans is now occupied by chalets.

Limeslade Bay, 1955.

Pennard village, bustling with activity, 1955.

Three Cliffs Bay, Gower, 1960.

TIMES OF TOIL

The glassworks, Loughor, early 1900s.

Cockle gatherers at Penclawdd, 1906.

The staff of Swansea prison, 1911. The central seated figure is prison governor Frank Walker Gibson. The picture was taken during a presentation to the white moustached man on the right of the governor who was the prison doctor, David Howell Thomas, probably to mark his retirement.

Pressdee's Motor Garage, Mumbles, was one of the area's main providers of taxis in and around the village in 1914. The vehicle on the right – a Napier – was contracted to the Admiralty at this time shortly before the outbreak of the First World War.

Sally Sawdust was the nickname of this woman who collected sawdust from the timber yards and sold it to places such as pubs and butchers shops for their floors. She is pictured here in the mid-1920s.

The fish wharf at Swansea, mid-1920s.

These men – and some youngsters – gathered at the crypt of St Paul's Church, Neath Road, Plasmarl, to peel potatoes for local soup kitchens during the 1926 General Strike.

Construction of the Prince of Wales dry dock, 1928.

Proprietor of Pressdee's Motor Garage Mr W. Pressdee, takes a break from his labours to be photographed with a Dodge car – one of his latest additions perhaps – in 1928.

Dawnays Structural Engineering Company employees at their Crymlyn Burrows works, 1929.

Hafod School teachers, 1932.

A builder checks his work with a straight edge, near Kimberley Road, Sketty, mid-1930s.

Fire wardens at Mumbles, 1939. they had commandeered both the garage and this Austin 20 vehicle to act as their fire engine.

Female staff of Snipper & Goldman, tailors, St Helen's Road, 1947.

Almost the entire workforce of the Windsmoor clothing factory, Fforestfach, turned out for this 1947 picture.

The staff of outfitters Sidney Heath's maids and boys department at their Walter Road shop, May 1949.

Miners at Garngoch No.3 Colliery, Penllergaer, early-1950s.

Workers playtime at Richard Thomas & Baldwin's Landore works, early-1950s.

Tir John Power Station, Port Tennant, mid-1950s.

An order checker at the office of Hancock's wines and spirits stores, York Street, mid-1950s.

Rebuilding the No.3 turbine at Tir John power station, Port Tennant, 1951.

Hodges menswear factory staff, Fforestfach, 1951.

Health visitors at Cwmbwrla clinic, December 1952.

Violet Ace, licensee of The Fairfield
Club with her son Glyn, 1954.

Members of the personnel records section at the borough treasurer's department Swansea Guildhall, June, 1954.

The borough treasurer's department, Swansea Guildhall, July 5, 1955.

The office of John Richards, wholesale grocers, Union Street, February, 1955.

A staff meeting at Gregg High School, Heathfield, 1955.

A porter with his trolley on Platform Two at Swansea High Street Station, 1957.

Telegram boys Brian Watkins, Rowland Page and Derek Tucker share a joke astride a BSA Bantam motorcycle at their Rutland Street office, 1957.

Workers at the Remploy factory, Fforestfach, late 1950s.

Mr D.G. Atwell, undertaker, with two of his assistants, early 1961. The firm also supplied wedding vehicles, hence the white ribbons on the bonnet of the car behind them.

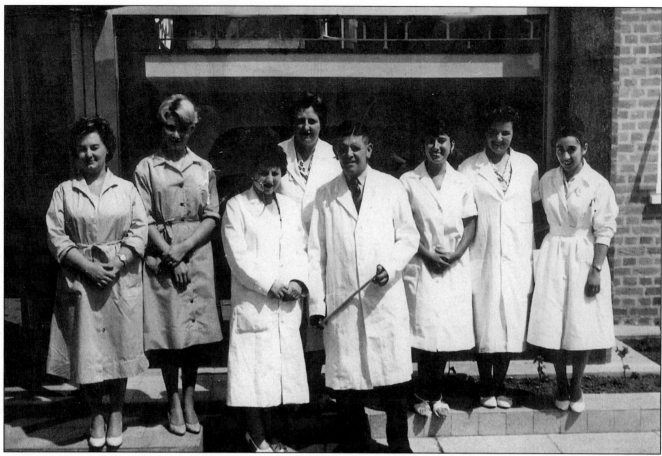

Staff of Singleton Hospital X-Ray department, June 21, 1961.

Regulars at The Tredegar Arms public house, Sandfields, keep the landlord busy in the early 1960s.

A group of Swansea-based steel erectors pose with the boss and his new Ford Zephyr Four saloon car, 1965.

Student nurses at the outpatients department, Singleton Hospital, 1966.

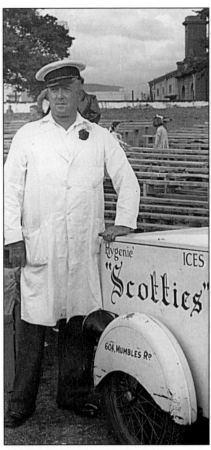

Ice cream vendor James Brown at St Helen's cricket ground, 1967.

Staff of Swansea's Mettoy factory with manager Paul Williams at temporary accommodation used by the firm at Skewen, 1972.

Staff of the Viscose factory at South Dock celebrate the firm's 75th anniversary, 1977.

Firemen take a welcome break from fighting a fire at Princess House office block, Princess Way, 1978. They are station officer Bob Rees, sub-officer B. Gates and fireman P. Dart of white watch, West Glamorgan Fire Service, Swansea.

Staff of Morriston Senior Comprehensive School, 1980.

TRAVEL AND TRADE

Passengers wait to board a train at Penclawdd railway station, 1899.

A wagon and horses prepares to convey its passengers from the Commercial Inn – at the junction of Eaton Road and Llangyfelach Road, Brynhyfryd – to Swansea, 1900.

Sailing vessels in the North Dock, mingle with their replacements, 1904.

More vessels in the North Dock, this time looking towards St Thomas, 1905.

Loading coal at the North Dock hoists, 1907.

A horse-drawn funeral cortège outside the premises of D.G. Phillips, funeral furnishers, Dillwyn Street, 1909.

The *Luciana* was the first steamer to berth in King's dock, October 1909.

Pressdees, of Stanley Street, Mumbles operated livery stables before the arrival of their first car in 1909 – and this was it. Initially customers were advised when booking they could be served by either horse-drawn or motor transport.

A line-up of Swansea taxis and a Great Western Railway delivery lorry in Ivey Place, outside High Street station, 1910. It is now Station Yard.

The paddle steamer Glen Gower in Swansea Bay, 1925.

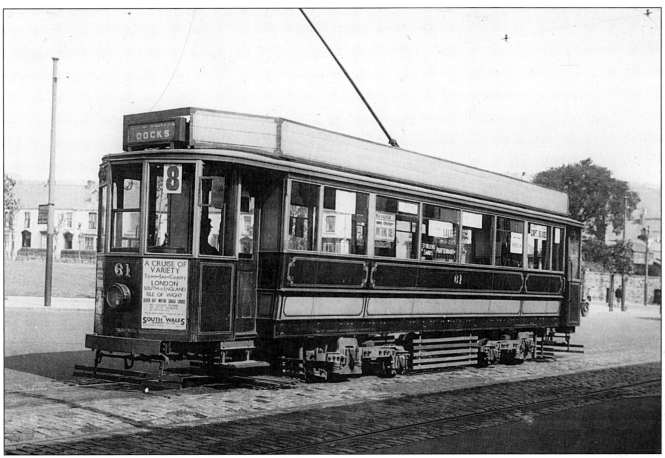

A single-deck tram of the Swansea Tramways & Improvements Company, outside its depot in St Helen's Road, early 1930s. Today it is the site of Swansea Crown Court.

A funeral coach outside D.G. Phillips & Son's undertakers at 208 Oxford Street, early 1930s.

Passengers leave a packed Mumbles train – steam hauled – on its return to Swansea. This picture was taken at The Slip. Hats certainly seem to have been the order of this sunny summer's day, 1910.

A hearse used by undertakers D.G. Phillips, of Oxford Street in the 1930s.

A busy King's Dock, 1930s.

A double-deck tram in Eversly Road, Sketty, 1932.

Jersey Marine airfield only operated for a short time in the late 1930s. flown in by De Havilland Dragon aircraft this is probably one of its most important passenger arrivals – Emperor Haille Sallase, of Abyssinia, front, in 1939. Shortly afterwards the Second World War broke out.

South Dock and the huge Coast Lines warehouse – now Swansea Maritime and Industrial Museum – alongside, early 1950s.

A horse drawn beer delivery dray used by William Hancock and Company, from its York Street depot, early 1950s.

The grain carrier Beekbergen berthed at Weaver's Flour Mills dock basin, 1951.

Wind Street high level railway junction and signal box, mid-1950s.

An AEC Regal III double decker waits outside the former Powell Duffryn building in Adelaide Street, to start its service on the number 73 route to Brynhyfryd via High Street station, mid-1950s.

A tug shepherds a cargo vessel to its berth in Swansea Docks, mid-1950s.

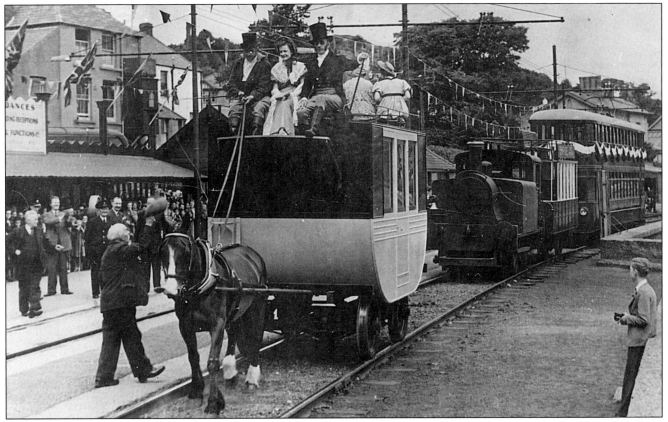

The three methods of propulsion used on the Mumbles Railway – two replicated for the event – came together for the line's 150th anniversary celebration in 1954. This picture was taken at Oystermouth Square.

Lorries were nowhere near the size they are today when this high-level picture of The Strand was taken in the mid-1950s.

An accident involving the Mumbles train and a motor vehicle at St Helen's on September 6, 1957.

Well, even youngsters had to have some kind of transport – and this was it pushchair style, 1959. the youngsters were snapped in Heol Fach, Treboeth.

Driver Len Manley and fireman Des Morgan turning a locomotive at Paxton Street engine sheds ready to work the 18.25 Swansea Victoria to York mail over the Central Wales line, early 1960s.

A train leaves Swansea Victoria station for Shrewsbury, in June 1961. The Guildhall clock tower can just be seen in the middle background.

Bracelet Bay car park – always a popular motorists rendezvous, 1963.

These were the lorries – and the men – who delivered for Annie Johns coal business in Danygraig, 1963.

The last passenger train to leave Swansea Victoria Station for Shrewsbury, on June 13, 1964. The locomotive hauling it was No.45406.

The Swansea-based wholesale confectionery firm of Roger Trollope shared its vehicle allegiance between Austin and Morris in 1973 as this picture shows.

TAKING A BREAK

There was plenty to do to pass the time on Swansea Sands in 1907. This picture was taken near the Slip bridge and shows the Bay View Hotel, back right, and passengers on the top deck of a passing Mumbles tram.

A Sunday school outing to Oxwich, on August 6, 1914.

A gathering of churchgoers on the beach at Langland, August 7, 1917.

Tulk's all-weather coach was just fine as transport for this outing of Swansea folk in 1930. The coach operators were based in Penfilia Road, Brynhyfryd.

The first car starting on the timber figure- eight railway built at Mumbles, early 1920s. It was later sold to Coney Beach, Porthcawl.

The family of well-known undertakers D.G. Phillips relax on a day out, mid-1930s.

A family picnic on Gower, late 1930s.

Enjoying the sun at Langland Bay, 1936.

Crymlyn Burrows was a popular venue at which to spend some time on the sands as this 1938 family snapshot shows.

A South Wales Transport staff outing, 1949.

Swansea Wesleyan Methodist Chapel Men's Guild trip, 1949.

A group of South Wales Transport conductresses all set for their annual outing, early 1950s.

Staff of the Geoff Davies Building Company, Paxton Street, Sandfields, on an annual outing to Blackpool, 1950.

Cwmbwrla tinplate workers get set for their annual excursion, 1950.

Employees of Richard Thomas & Baldwin's Landore works on an early 1950s day out.

The regatta at Mumbles certainly drew the crowds in 1952.

Employees of Potters Construction before embarking on a coach trip, 1952.

A Sunday school from Pentremawr Road, Hafod, at Caswell, on its annual outing, 1939.

Staff of Singer Sewing Machines, Swansea, on an outing to Llanwrtyd Wells, July 5, 1954.

Staff of the Lewis Lewis store all ready to depart for an excursion to Llandrindod Wells, mid-1950s.

This was just one of the displays that would have greeted visitors to the Gower Show at Penrice, in 1956.

Workers on A-shift at Tir John Power Station on an annual outing, mid-1950s.

Office staff from Woolworth's High Street store in high spirits during a 1962 day out.

Picking a card to send home – tourists at Langland Bay, Gower, July 1962.

This was one outing that didn't have a happy ending. The pleasure steamer Prince Ivanhoe, grounded off Porteynon, Gower, summer 1983 and sparked a full-scale rescue operation.

Senior citizens from Powys Avenue, Townhill, before setting out on a mystery tour, summer 1962.

THE ENTERTAINERS

Sketty Male Voice Party, 1909, with A.V. Jones, conductor.

St John's Church Choir, Gowerton in costume for the production of *Pearl the Fisher Maiden* which they staged in May 1914.

Members of The Carltons dance band ready to set off on an outing, mid-1920s.

Geoff and The Mandoliers, at Brynhyfryd Hall, 1930s.

Members of Sion chapel and St Paul's Church, Clydach when they performed the pantomime *Cinderella* at Clydach church hall, mid-1930s. The hall is now Clydach surgery.

Members of Uplands Arts Club take time out from the dress rehearsal for one of their popular late 1940s amateur productions.

The Manhattans dance band at the Casino, Newton Road, Mumbles, 1952. They provided the music there for 35 years.

The cast of *Dick Whittington*, a pantomime staged at West Cross Community Centre by Mrs Matthews who gathered children from the area for many similar productions in the mid-1950s.

Ready to march… members of Brynmelyn Street Comedy Band, Waun Wen, 1953.

The young actors club at Terrace Road School, 1959.

Members of the choir of the 53rd (Welsh) Division Company RASC (TA) gathered at the Drill Hall, Richardson Street, preparing to leave for a concert at the Royal Albert Hall, London, late 1950s.

Founder members of Swansea Philharmonic Choir at the National School, Oxford Street, in 1960. Included are conductor Haydn James along with many other well-known personalities. The choir was formed a year earlier.

Rehearsal time for members of Swansea Philharmonic Choir, mid-1960s. Included at extreme left, second row is Dilys Lloyd, organist at St Mary's parish church and wife of Morgan Lloyd, leader of the orchestra bearing his name.

Crowds gather in the then pedestrianised College Street to listen to a band of musical evangelists, mid-1960s.

The cast of Miranda, the 1960 offering from St Michael's Church Dramatic Society's, Manselton.

Peter Boyce, who took part in Night Must Fall, part of the Grand Theatre's repertory season, July, 1962. John Chilvers was the producer.

Brynhyfryd Chapel Band of Hope youngsters during a 1965 production.

British Railways, Swansea Victoria Male Voice Choir, comprised mostly of locomotive drivers, firemen and guards, January 9, 1966.

Scouts, Guides, Rangers and Venture Scouts in a 1970s Gang Show produced at the Grand Theatre by John Chilvers.

Members of Swansea Male Choir before leaving for a tour of Germany, 1972.

Trevor Roberts, a member of Swansea's popular Manhattans dance band still playing at the age of 86. Seen here at the British Legion Club Mumbles, in the mid-1970s.

West Glamorgan School Band, at Townhill Training College, April 12, 1975.

Sketty Park Gems jazz band at the World Jazz Band Championships, Birmingham, August, 1981.

Singleton Hospital drama group in a mid-1980s pantomime production.

PLAYING THE GAME

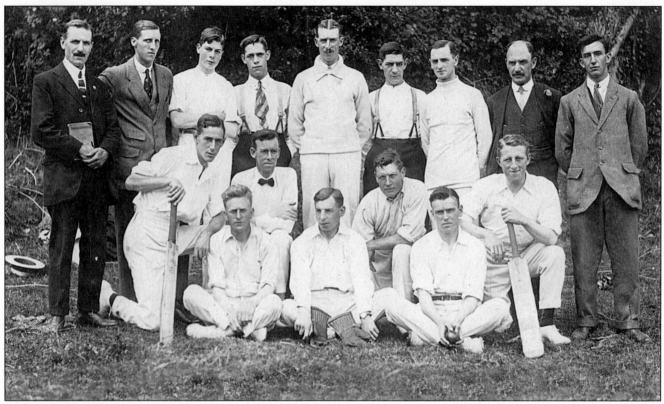

Oystermouth Athletic Cricket Club, 1919.

Hafod Brotherhood football team and officials, 1925-26.

Mayhill School Soccer squad, 1946.

St David's School football team, 1946-47.

Waiting for the off… entrants in the egg and spoon race at Hafod School sports day, 1947.

Hafod Junior School football team 1947-48.

Waun Wen AFC reserves, 1950 pictured with the trophies won by the first team.

Blackpill lads checking the score card astride a wartime pill box after an impromptu game of cricket, 1950.

Form 5a, Llwyn Y Bryn School, at Townhill playing fields, March 20, 1951.

Prime Minister Winston Churchill shakes the hand of former Swansea Town player Ray Daniels before the start of the 1952 Cup Final. Daniels, a Welsh international, by then was playing for Arsenal.

Llwyn Y Bryn School's sixth form on Swansea Beach near the slip for hockey practice, January 29, 1952.

A judo class held alongside war-damaged Swansea Grammar School, early 1950s.

Townhill School football team, 1952.

Gors Junior School – Swansea Schools, League champions, 1952.

Tower United football team, 1953.

Tower United at Vetch Field, 1954.

The football team at Richard Thomas & Baldwin's, Landore works, 1954.

Anyone for tennis? These women – pictured at Victoria Park on April 15, 1955 worked at the nearby Guildhall – certainly were.

Members of the Swansea Ministry of Pensions and National Insurance office cricket team, 1958.

Bonymaen Athletic football team and officials outside the New Inn, Bonymaen, 1958.

Members of the gymnastics club at Terrace Road School, 1959.

Bonymaen RFC, late 1950s.

Clarence United, 1961. Their activities were centred on Clarence Street, Sandfields.

Clase School football team 1967-68.

John Glover, right, was the winner of the annual Mumbles to Aberavon swim, 1964.

Newton School, Mumbles, netball team, 1984.

Newton School, Mumbles, netball squad, 1986.